Weaving the Wind

poems by

Antoinette Voûte Roeder

apocryphile press
BERKELEY, CA

Apocryphile Press
1700 Shattuck Ave #81
Berkeley, CA 94709
www.apocryphile.org

Printed in the United States of America.
ISBN 1-933993-08-1

For Nicholas, Sasha, and Rita
poets all
and
for all who have mentored me

acknowledgments

I wish to thank the following periodicals, newsletters, and their editors, for having published the poems listed below.

"Spiritual Direction Moment" originally published in *Connections: Newsletter of Spiritual Directors International*, Winter 1994.

"Here to Stay" originally published in *Pacific Church News: Magazine of the Episcopal Church in the San Francisco Bay Area*, Spring 2002.

"Daffodils" originally published in *Pacific Church News*, Spring 2003.

"The Labyrinth" originally published in *Pacific Church News*, Autumn 2005.

"Cana Wine" originally published as "Cana" in *Presence: The Journal of Spiritual Directors International,* September 1995.

"The Sower" originally published in *Presence*, January 1999.

"Treasure in the Field" originally published in *Presence*, May 2000.

"Day After Day" originally published in *Presence*, June 2002.

"The Last Act" originally published in *Presence*, June, 2003.

"Afternoon" originally published in *Quest: Journal of St. Stephen's College*, United Church of Canada, Spring 1995.

"Spiritual Direction" originally published in *Quest*, Fall 1995.

"Breath (2)" originally published in *Reaching Out with Yoga: The Magazine of Sharing Ideas, Expanding Knowledge, and Creating Community*, No. 7.

"Tree Pose" originally published in *Reaching Out with Yoga*, No. 10.

"Beloved" originally published as "Prayer, a different version" in *Reaching Out with Yoga*, No. 11.

"Breath (1)" originally published in *Yoga Bridge: Newsletter of the Yoga Association of Alberta*, Spring 2001.

All biblical quotes and references are taken from *The New Oxford Annotated Bible with the Apocryphal/Deuterocanonical Books: the New Revised Standard Version*, edited by Bruce M. Metzger and Roland E. Murphy, 1991, New York: Oxford University Press.

Photo Credits:
Cover photo of Rochon Sands Provincial Park, Alberta, by Nicholas Andrew Roeder.

Author photo by Aldo Voûte

"And for all this, nature is never spent;
There lives the dearest freshness deep down things...."

God's Grandeur by Gerard Manley Hopkins

"The wind blows where it chooses,
and you hear the sound of it, but you do not know
where it comes from or where it goes."

John 3:8

contents

Introduction 13

I. The Garden…did we ever leave it?

Zen Garden Poems 21
Garden..23
Garden Memories 24
Sabbath Bath...25
Rain 26
West Coast Winter...27
cloud 29
One 31
Fall 32
Keeping the Faith 33
Afternoon 34
Geese..36
Solstice Walk 37
Restoration 39
Ravine...40
Related...41
Theophany 42
Psalm..43
February in Kananaskis 44
On this winter morning..45
Soundings...46
Breaking Open..47
Waxwings 48
Life at the Edge...49

Justice 50
Atlantic 51
Wild Life 52
A Day of Geese 53
The Great Horned Owl 54
Thermal 55
Coyote 56
thirty seconds of mouse 57
Hare 58
Beholding 59
Stillness 60
Life 61
Cartesian Non-Sense 62
Lament 63
New Lease 64

II. "What are you doing here, Elijah?"

First 67
Day 68
And God Said 69
I wonder if 70
Welcome 71
Work 73
Spiritual Direction Moment 74
Outside/Inside 75
The Sower 76
Spiritual Direction 77
Treasure in the Field 78
Guru 79
gifts 80
Voices 81
Tree Pose 82

Breath (1) 83
Oblation 84
I am 85
not a word 86
Godbearer 87
Cana Wine 89
I will not worship you 91
Holy 93
Here to Stay 95
Daffodils 96
Choose Life 97
Litany 99
Journey 101
what magdalene heard 103
The Labyrinth 104
People Who Sit 105
Beloved 106
Sitting 107
Contemplation 108
Take my heart 109
A Poet's Prayer 110
Prayer at Providence 111
Breath (2) 112
unconsoled 113
all 114
Organic Breath 115
Spirit 116
Day after day 117
Spaciousness 118
"Vast emptiness, nothing holy" 119
"What are you doing here, Elijah?" 120
Nameless 121
Promise 122

III. To write or not to write

Gift for a Writer 125
Plath and Sexton 126
Other Voices 127
protesting poet 128
For Denise Levertov 129
summer eucharist 130
Poetry Time 131
Night Rain 132
To write or not to write 133
Poems 134
Natalie 135
Poem 137
Attendance 138
Inner Poet 139
The Power of Poetry 140
Poet Laureate 141
Poetry and Poets 142
A Reading 143
Food 144
Too Many Ghosts 145

IV. The seasons of my life

Spring Geese 149
April 150
Siberian Spring 151
Tulips 152
Berries 153
Dawn 154
After the Flood 155

July oh-four 156
Swimmer 157
Turning Sixty 158
Fallow Field 159
Advent 160
Free for Christmas 161
New Mexico 163
Done 165
Who I Am 166
Oyster 167
Free 168
Mountain 169
Mystics 170
Less 171
Star 172
Daft 173
Don't look to me 175
What, not Why 176
Convention 177
Death or Life? 179
Escape 180
War Chant 182
Companion 183
Death 184
Morning and Evening Poems 186
Tree 187
Exhale 188
Passion 189
The Last Act 190

About the Author 192

introduction

Language and words have been a source of delight and play for me for a long time. I wonder, though, whether that would have been the case had I not been forced to learn a new language when I was ten years old.

Our family emigrated from Holland to the oilfields of southern New Mexico two months before my tenth birthday. This is where my writing career started. I wrote letters. I developed a flourishing correspondence with uncles and aunts and family friends left behind in the old country. It was my way of staying connected with the known and the comfortable. What *they* lived back home was real. What *I* was experiencing was surely fantasy. I could not find my footing in this alien landscape, culture, and lifestyle.

Where I *could* be comfortable was in my head. I was intent on learning my second language and actually enjoyed the weekly list of vocabulary words we had to spell, define, and use correctly. I liked using some of the more unusual words in my conversations. How insufferable I must have seemed to my classmates! I even went so far as to correct my teachers. Everyone knows that is *verboten*. What a little upstart!

By the time I was in high school we had made two more moves. In high school English I was exposed to great literature and poetry. I was still writing letters but had also delved into writing love stories, incredibly sentimental and highly unlikely love stories. I dared present these to my English teacher who, in his spare time, took the trouble to look them over and comment on them. I still have the stories as well as his comments, written in the margins in red ink. Mr. Zellefrow saw some promise in me and suggested I try my hand at poetry. "Keep searching for the exact word or phrase," he said. And, "There is always the danger of saying too much in poetry." He took me seriously as a writer and a person and his support was seminal in my development. I am very grateful to him.

Poetry fit me like a glove. I never wrote stories again, I never looked back. Here was something real into which I could pour my heart and soul.

"The wind blows where it chooses, and you hear the sound of it, but you do not know where it comes from or where it goes" (John 3). I have always loved this verse from John's gospel. I cannot grasp the wind anymore than I can capture the essence of poetry. Nevertheless, my poetry is an attempt to hold on to the wind, to ride its coattails if only for a second, and to put words to that experience. It slips through my fingers. Like a prism, it breaks into different colors, all fluid. So much depends on what is *not* said, on the spaces between the words, and on the silence from which they emerge.

So much depends on the reader and what you bring to it. Every reading of a poem may reveal something new, something different from before. That is equally true for the poet. She may come back to her own poem some time later and see in it things she did not know were there. Poetry is never done. It is a living form.

Good poetry changes us. I have looked up from such a poem and known that I am seeing through different eyes. It may be microscopic change but it is very real. Why else do totalitarian regimes round up poets and writers if not for the fact that they recognize the power the written word has to change people?

Poetry is akin to prayer for me. It requires the same deeply quiet, receptive mode. In prayer I meet the wind that blows where it will. In John's gospel that wind refers to the Spirit or the Breath of the Holy. I cannot know that Breath, that Mystery, except by the deep yearning of my heart. But I believe that Breath has breathed everything into being and my poetry is, if it is anything, an act of love to the Creative Breath.

The poets who have influenced me most and whom I read over and over are Mary Oliver, Robert Frost, and Gerard Manley Hopkins. (A second tier of three would be Wendell Berry, T.S. Eliot, and R. M. Rilke.) Of those three, Frost is the most sober. He keeps me in check. Hopkins is the ecstatic. I cannot resist the music and the vision of his poesy. Mary Oliver is the poet for my daily consumption. Her love of and delight in the natural world, her awareness of the sacred, are like bread for me. One of the poems in this collection speaks to that fact.

This collection represents years of poetizing. Some of these poems were published, most were not. When I read through them I see that the subject matter remains more or less the same throughout. Nature, mystery, spirituality, and writing itself have been my themes. They are the things that have inspired me. As I grew a little bolder, injustice, greed, and the degradation of our earth evoked my voice. With that voice came a greater awareness of my embodied self and a radical awakening to the fact that I am made of the earth's stuff. What affects the earth affects me. What I do affects the earth.

In my thirties, I started reading Pierre Teilhard de Chardin. In him I found a man of deep faith and religious conviction who combined the soul of a mystic with a scientific mind, a man who appreciated the rich gifts of our earth and the deep mysteries of the cosmos. It was probably the beginning of my understanding of what I like to call "the seamless garment." To me the garment of Christ, for which the soldiers gambled at the foot of the cross, symbolizes the un-separability of things. I comprehend that on the mystical level and now, quantum physics has come up with proof that it is indeed so. All in the universe relates and connects and interconnects. The whole earth system is therefore incredibly vulnerable because, as John Donne put it so beautifully centuries ago, "No man is an island." Today we would expand on that to include the entire natural order. If the natural order is so inextricably bound together, there are consequences when one aspect of it breaks down. For a long, long time the earth was able to absorb those consequences. With the population explosion and rampant greed, that seems no longer possible. What the earth suffers and will suffer, we also suffer. That is the cost of interconnectedness.

Nature, its inherent right to be what it is, is a passion of mine. I see it as an extension of my passion for the Holy, for the spirituality of life lived at its source, for music and poetry and people. It is the seamless garment.

I have had a life-long love affair with music. Music has been the continuum, my mainstay, and sometimes, the only way by which I still knew myself. I grew up in a musical family, a household in which music-making and listening were as natural as breathing. I started piano lessons when I was five years old and never quit studying music, through a graduate degree and more than a quarter century of teaching piano. You may hear echoes of music in my poetry, the delight in sound, rhythm, and cadence. A late mid-life shift occurred when I became interested in a greater understanding and experience of the Spirit. I sought out a spiritual director who guided me through the Spiritual Exercises of St. Ignatius of Loyola, a deep and life-changing practice of prayer. I was taken by surprise when I felt called to become a spiritual guide to others. I had imagined myself teaching piano into old age. Instead, I took a sabbatical year from teaching in order to follow a training and formation program in spiritual direction and have been doing that privileged work for the last fifteen years. Though I no longer teach piano, most days I still make time to practice and play. There is nothing like making music oneself. I believe that the deep listening to music which I learned over the years provided the groundwork for the deep listening I do in spiritual direction, as well as in writing. They come from the same well.

My friends and my family have always shown interest in my poetry, encouraging me, confirming my gifts. But no one has been so wholeheartedly supportive as John Mabry, my publisher. He has formed a cheering section of one that can be heard clear across the playing field! My greatest fan, over the past decade he has published me wherever he could, in his capacity as editor. I am honored that he has agreed to take this volume on. To John, then, a deep Zen bow.

I hope I have not "said too much." As I grow older, I prefer fewer words. Gone are the arabesques of an overactive romanticism. Everything shakes out to the sparse and the spare.

May you find meaning in these pages. May we live to love, honor, and respect each other and the earth.

Shalom.

i. the garden…
did we ever leave it?

zen garden poems

I

Bee
dug deep
in yellow poppy

research
for a bee's degree

poppy sways
from side to side
bee sits undisturbable

ah
to be so clad,
so nestled
in a poppy's yellow cup

II

Bee
intent on
poppy work
receives a visit
from a fly

Shoo!

III

Bee has left
her golden cradle

poppy trembles
at the loss

garden

Wandering the paths
of this graceful garden
I stop to cradle the waxy blooms
of a spreading magnolia tree.
The rhododendrons dress in pink,
fiery red, and tender mauve.
Cedars so tall I can't see their crowns
dance with small bushes and lower still,
midnight-purple speckled bells
bow their heads to the rich black earth.

The garden gives way
to a building, a chapel.
Its interior is dim,
it sounds hollow inside,
exudes a musty smell.
Windows and wood
hold static space.
Jesus, are you here?

I can't be sure
but *this* I know:
out there between scraggly wild heather
and bunches of buttery marsh marigolds,
under the fragrant flowering arbutus,
God walks in the cool of the morning.

garden memories

In the garden
deeply breathing
through my eyes

In the garden
heart suspended
softened sounds

In the garden
limitless body
all is flow

In the garden
life itself
bears me away

The garden…
did we ever leave it?

sabbath bath

With the rumble of rain
thick on summer foliage
richly canopied over the garden,
a sibilant chorus of leaves
mingled with the robin's champagne song
and the steady hum of water
dribbling down the drainpipe,
I recline in my own watery oasis,
window open on the garden
and through me flows another water,
ancient sea of our origins,
and the inner sea that was my cradle
before the world sped me away.

Timeless rain and ageless water
gather in my body's book,
diary of nature's making.
They conspire to take me back
to the stuff of my creation,
to the One who dreamed it all.

rain

evening's deluge
morning's whisper
rain

sweet attire
for parched earth
rain

morning prayer
a single candle
walls fall down
rain

west coast winter

Winter on the west coast
        unfolds, takes hold
when the grey sky slumps
        into the sea,
slips over wet earth
        matted with leaves,
and colors blend, bleed wet-wood hues
        of muted mustard,
                cranberry and rust.

I walk among the silent trees
whose finely tangled twigs and branches
terminate in globes so small:
        raindrops loath to fall
        and yet not grasping,
suspended easily between earth and sky.

It's comforting, this leaky quilt
of heavy cloud, this grey silk
cover drawing me into
its copious cushions, shrinking
the world to safer dimensions,
dependable in its predictability:
        rain today,
                and yesterday,
                        and likely tomorrow as well.

West coast winter unfolds,
        takes hold and settles in.
I tramp its windblown leafy paths

and scan its soggy shoreline.
Under its gently persistent tutelage
I soften into shapes
of greater receptivity,
modes of moist creativity,
more wholly at home on planet earth
and grateful guest of the universe.

cloud

If I were to come
  this way again
could it be
  as a cloud this time?
The ultimate shape-
  shifters, color-catchers,
clouds reach and reflect
  the hidden places
of canyon and summit,
never disclosing their secrets.

They wrap around mountains
  and huddle
in their more misty guise
on rivers and lakes,
in valleys and fields.
They travel in silence
alone or in crowds
over every imaginable
feature of earth.
They lack nothing
nor do they possess.

Measured in miles
  or nothing but
  a thin wisp of wool,
clouds disappear in the end:
    evaporate,
        rain themselves out
            or simply fail to form

and that would be all right
  with me
if I were to come this way again
  and this time as a cloud.

one

I looked at the sunset
until its peach
had burnt into molten
white gold that poured
itself out behind
my eyes and flowed,
flowed through my body,
turning each cell into
sunset sky.

fall

When the noonday sun
penetrates
the retreating chill of morning,
day is suspended,
a drop of bronze warmth,
liquid amber....

No memory of yesterday
nor thought of tomorrow,
I live in this moment,
newly created and one with
the stately dark evergreens,
delicate blonde birches,
the faded streaked sky.

Autumn...
more peaceful, more stable
than spring in its rawness,
boisterous summer or
forbidding winter.

Fall...
mature, mellow,
the pinnacle of the year
and its crown.

keeping the faith

Stepping outside
one early evening
on the first day of fall
we hear them, high,
high overhead and look
and see them, bending
in southeasterly direction,
geese, hundreds of geese,
casting themselves before the clouds,
one signature after another scrawled
across the pinking sky,
barking each other into line,
lines so fluid, constantly changing
yet always faithful to the design.

Higher than high
heading into the night
they urge each other,
trusting the stars, their ancient
heritage, instinctive witnesses
to the sacred, to interplay
of time and space, to mystery written
into the heart of things.

afternoon

In the aftermath of autumn,
or rather,
in the late afternoon of the year,
surprise:

> Surprise of birches
> Blooming,
> Their frothy network of delicate branches
> Etched
> Against a late northern sunrise sky
> Streaked in charcoal and rose.
>
> Surprise of birds,
> A flock of them rising
> Like scattered smoke
> In silent flight
> On the wings of the hospitable air.
>
> Surprise of berries
> In bunches,
> Clutches of scarlet and flame;
> On their own at last
> Now that leaves have disappeared.

And I who delighted in trees
robed in costumes so dazzling
they robbed me of breath
stand enraptured,
eyes open to glory
of Other and unexpected.

Surprised by Creation
so wondrously wrought,
so constantly changing,
so exposed and so spare,
so gifted and giving
so late in the year.

geese

The feathered, flapping waters writhe
with geese gathering, shatter
into sharp shards of light
breaking on the lake.

The wild mystery of yearly migration
is about to begin
with waterfowl massing
and family groups
taking their practice flights.

Here they come now
midst dissonant squawking
flippered feet thrashing, flashing orange
apparently running on the lake surface
till wings lift weight
and blessed air
carries them over the treetops.

Daily they drill
raucous and quarrelsome
till suddenly everyone
disappears.
Silence lies heavy upon the lake.

Later, trekking home ourselves,
we spot a massive "V" above.

Safe journey south, brave travelers.
God speed you on your way.

solstice walk

On the shortest day of the year the sun hangs waist-high amid spruces and pines, casting a coppery glow on the snow. We paddle laboriously through drifts, heaving up, sinking down upon a trail we know is there but whose contours have been all but swallowed up in the folds of winter's quilt.

A thin finger of land rides the river like a kayak. The river has turned to stone. A lone dry snag stands slightly apart, a scout for its healthier cousins. The osprey watched, in warmer times, from one of its withered arms. Does it miss its regal resident? It had dignity then. Now it is merely a long-dead tree trunk, shivering in the cold. Around the bend, a tall, thin post bears the chaotic osprey nest. It sits empty and quiet, sure of spring and the return of its builders.

More than one tree lies limbs akimbo on the forest floor, ravished by a mighty wind. Roots exposed and studded with pebbles, they tear ragged wounds in the undisturbed snowskin that surrounds them. Twiggy trees and lanky bushes braid their lengthening shadows ahead on the path. Like rungs of a ladder, they mark our way, silently closing ranks behind us.

I love this walk. I love the Wedgwood-blue sky above, its relentless cold as hard as the river below. I love the familiar landmarks that winter disguises, transforming them into mysterious strangers. I love the dollops of snow bearing down on the evergreens' branches. They remind me of elephant feet, so big are they. I'm exhilarated by the joy of discovery and exploration, by the cutting edge of the crystal-flecked air and the freshness of the landscape. It pleases me to plunge my boots in deep powder and haul them out again with each step.

Soon this short afternoon will meld with the longest night, bringing with it deep darkness and a splash of stars. All that will remain of this day are a fleeting taste, an unmapped movement, an indistinct form passing behind the eyes. Tomorrow our journey back to the sun begins.

restoration

The forest smells like Christmas.
Its pungent scent evokes a shudder
of pleasure until we stumble upon
fir boughs fanned across the snow
and further on, hundreds of trees
felled, like shipwrecks strewn
on the forest floor.

Where they are cut,
so clean, so clinical,
their honeyed insides ooze.
Age and effort, their laborious growth,
their juiciness, count for nothing
where they lie. Hundreds of logs,
long and straight and
dead and neatly stacked.
Nothing but a lumberjack's dream.

Take a tree down. Plant a sign.
(Signs persuade, signs sell.)
Signs announce the project:
to restore balance
to these fire-prone woods.

Ravens pour out of the sky,
their raucous cries a mournful sound.

Poor Mother Nature.
Where would she be
without our constant intervention.

ravine

Trudging through the deep
ravine the snow is polished,
packed down hard
beneath my boots.
In mid-afternoon
on this wintry day
the washed-out sun
pours itself out
towards the horizon
at my back
while a two-thirds moon
wobbles weakly ahead
grazing the canyon's edge.
Between sun and moon
with cold shadows swelling
I am adrift in a sea of snow,
soon to vanish with the dark.

related

In the stillness that breathes
between darkness and dawn
a single planet hangs over Mt. Kidd.
The mountain glimmers,
dressed in a fine new cover of snow.

A luminous planet,
who knows how distant,
appears here in our pre-dawn sky;
the far and the near inextricably bound
as are all things in the universe.

Were we ever to awaken
to the reality of our connection
chains would drop,
our imprisonment end.
Alive with wonder,
love would find us
as if for the very first time.

Mt. Kidd is a peak in Kananaskis Country, Alberta.

theophany

It was an ordinary walk
on a sun-flecked day
with clouds sparring for space
in a roomy blue sky.
A powdery snow lay about between
maize-colored grasses and rust-red bushes.
Quiet covered the valley.

A solitary raven caught our attention
telling a story of ravendom,
a tale of deep gurgles, clucks,
and near-human wails,
bouncing off the mountain sides.

Something broke open inside of me
as unannounced tears flowed
and somewhere within me
someone knelt down
before a burning bush.

psalm

Praise Him for the glaciers:
grizzled, grey, forbidding,
glazed with an aqua glow
at every chasm and crevasse.
        Praise God for the heights.

Praise Her for the forest floor covered
with the silk of larch needles,
dull gold in the October sun.
Praise Her for the lone hawk
soaring high over the dark abyss
between Mt. Temple and Mt. Sheol.
        Praise God for the depths.

Praise Him for an azure sky
reflected in a turquoise lake,
for the quiet and the silence
and communion of the summits.

Above all, praise Her for unseen mysteries,
the beauties of the world
hidden from human eyes.
Their very existence is their right to be
and gives pleasure to our God.
        Let all Creation praise the Lord.

february in kananaskis

Mid-winter sun
catches hold of a snowfield
slanting off the mountainside,
coaxes it into giving itself
away in lazy wisps
lighter than smoke, than
the sheerest breath of cloud.

High mountain country hosts
all kinds of weather,
changing from moment to moment.
Before the next storm
rolls through the valley,
snow lapping up every crag and meadow,
I wed myself to
this impermanent beauty
as it evaporates before my eyes

...and if I were
to evaporate with it,
then that would be
all right as well.

on this winter morning

On this winter morning
a sunrise of old rose
and lavender is layered
band by band upon
the far edge of the world.

Feathered fingers of naked trees
reach into this pastel blossoming
as if hoping to procure
some of the color for their own.

Not till spring weaves her way back
will they be clothed in anything
as lovely as this morning sky.

soundings

In the mountains
I hear the sky
pour itself out
over silent peaks.

Absence of sound
makes its own sound.

Sometimes I know
I hear in the sky
the *fiat* of
Creation.

breaking open

As if cut out
of the cobalt sky,
the mountain's granite edges shimmer.

Below
a creamy butterfly
dances among fringed blooms,
a field of yellow dandelions.

It's enough to break your heart
wide open.

waxwings

A bundle of birds
flashes through the sky
wheeling and floating
silvery one moment
the next a dull grey.
Erupting from nowhere
they vanish as quickly,
the peripatetic waxwings.

Sometimes they decorate a spruce
sitting like balls on a Christmas tree.
Facing the setting sun they sit
seemingly cast in stone.
Other times they rain
from the branches, wave upon wave
silent except for the *swoosh*
of their flight.
They are a sure sign
of serious winter,
messengers from up north.
They will be
our faithful companions
till milder weather
warms our land.

life at the edge

Life at the edge
for the slim-stilted heron
means slow-poking around
in shallow sea,
impossibly intent,
giraffe-like neck
ready to spring,
oblivious to water
lapping its legs.

Each wave wreaks havoc
with its perfect reflection
not unlike a circus mirror.
But even if it could,
the great blue heron
would never laugh,
being far too dignified
a bird.

justice

A crab
the size of a small dinner plate
dangles haphazardly
from the gull's yellow bill.
Legs flailing,
it will not escape.
Repeatedly dashed
against the rocks
to break its shell,
it quickly becomes
a meal.

No pan,
no fire,
no fine moral qualms
but a peculiar justice
as the hungry are fed.

I'd rather watch
a gull eat a crab
than sit down myself
at a linen-laid table
to consume this tasty crustacean.

atlantic

Standing as if rooted on this rock
before an ageless sea,
time and space blend truly,
bend in this vast ocean
as it clings to a spinning globe
that circles ever in space.

It presents itself without apology,
this sea,
neither friendly nor un. It *is*, and
it is I who have to find my footing
in a place that is all water and sky.

Here I meet a history not mine,
encounter an alien worldscape,
catch a glimpse of overwhelming forces
that formed this water
when the human was but a dream.

The ocean pays me no heed.
Even now it breathes its origins
as it fills this moment
and flows into the next:
        ancient voice,
                cosmic sage.

wild life

No vestige of legs,
there is only a body
floating on this algae-pocked pond.
He stands immobile,
the great blue heron,
immensely patient,
his whole being an exclamation
of wholly focused intensity.

Slowly the muscular neck unravels,
suavely spiraling over the water,
leaving the rest of his body behind.
His head plunges down
through the opaque surface.
With a lightning strike
of his bright scissored bill,
a tiny black fish squirms helplessly
between its powerful blades.
A gulp, a swallow,
and what breathed life
now knots within
the spaghetti-stretched throat.

Unruffled, unwaffled,
the heron resumes
his silent watch
over quiet waters
as rain begins
to fall.

a day of geese

Mid morning sky breaks into smudges,
groups of Canada geese are flying
towards the open lake.
If up too high, they keel over,
one after another, wings drooping
to break their speed, to land where they intended.
Foraging, preening, an occasional squabble,
keep them busy throughout the day.

At sun's descent they start to pace.
They mutter, grumble and plough the air
with wings deployed and powerful.
At a certain moment known only to them,
they gather. Clusters rise, one at a time,
cheered on by instructional honking.

The lake remains behind alone.
Darkness covers her like a quilt.

the great horned owl

The elder statesman of the forest,
hair neatly combed in lateral tufts
wears a herringbone vest and fine striped socks
and speaks in dulcet tones,
white beard bobbing as his wide tail lifts.

He is quite the gentleman
except perhaps when his great gold eyes
fix upon yours, quite unabashed,
and his feet, those flashy claws,
hook into their helpless prey.

The great horned owl
does nothing halfway,
is fastidious in feeding,
wasting nothing:
  bones and feathers,
  fur and whiskers,
  all is processed
  into pellets
  that he spits
  upon the ground.

When he flies
his wings billow out
like a bustled skirt.
He spirals through trees
with his all-seeing gaze,
formidable presence
to lesser folk.

thermal

Here they come
in orderly fashion
marching neatly
across the sky
when…
what is this chaos,
this melee,
this sudden, senseless muddle?

Goose bumps goose
brushes aside its fellows,
each competing for a chance
to fly the labyrinth.

It's a thermal
and oh, the ride!
What joy, what ecstasy!
One by one they join the spinning,
spiraling higher, climbing the sky.

Just as suddenly,
without warning
each melts away,
bows out of the dance.
Now so high,
they are mere specks.
Specks as orderly
as before, form
and reform, fly
away, gracefully sailing
out of sight.

coyote

Padding out of the trees
one early winter afternoon
catching the earth-hugging sun
in the tips of her tawny fur,
she moves silently over
the yellow grass poking
stubbornly through
a thin crust of snow.

Her elegant bush of a tail
ends in handsome black fringe,
balancing the long thin snout
she carries low to the ground.
Her coat is luxurious,
  heavy and thick,
maize blending to beige and gold,
  colors reflecting the terrain.

She sniffs the air,
  hesitates slightly,
then with springy step
moves away, so fluid,
so perfectly what she is,
giving glory to God
with every muscle,
with every cell of her being.

thirty seconds of mouse

A wide expanse
of snow-padded path
suddenly shivers
into life.
A very small ball
of charcoal-grey fur
followed by
an absurdly long tail
hurries toward us
hugging the side.

It stops by my boot,
(big, brown, and clumsy)
cocks its head
so I see its bright eye,
then glides away swiftly
up the walk of a house
and slips out of sight
in the crack by the step.

Here and gone,
thirty seconds of mouse.
The frozen land
has come alive
with the flash of a miniscule miracle.

hare

When I rise from prayer
 and open my drapes
he sits immobile across the street
 like a discarded paper bag.
He lounges in grass grown tall,
 midst a generous scattering
of weeds.

Rooting around, he snaps off a leaf
 and munches methodically,
stem to stern.
 The bloom of a dandelion
meets the same fate: first
 the long stem, then the flower,
a yellow button, poised momentarily
 on his nose before it vanishes
down his throat.

 While I sat earnestly on my knees
 struggling with my life and the holy,
 he on his knees, sunk into the grass,
 was feasting under the sky.

He *is* prayer.
I labor at it.

beholding

Early Sunday late August morning
and the geese are coming,
    straggling, straying, braying,
        cheering,
a mosaic of masks and lanky length
in flight.

I stop to salute
our shared origins
in the galactic dust, in
bills and feathers, skin and hair
whose blueprint has vanished
over the course
of eons.

Every thing eventually draws me
into sacred mystery
where boundaries dissolve
in the simplicity of beholding.

stillness

The early fog
lilts and lifts
rolls and rises
in perfect silence.

The mountain stands
as morning sun
melts night's shadows
in perfect silence.

The grebe returns
strong feet paddling
sailing the watery surface
in perfect silence.

Sometimes silence gives birth to stillness
but stillness is present in another way.

The fog, the mountain, the grebe
are.
Stillness lies at the heart of essence.
When stillness finds me
eternity unfolds.

life

What is life? or
what is truth? as Pilate asked.

The early morning grebe
pops up through placid water
ruffling the reflection.

He dives deep, leaves a ring
that keeps on growing.
What does he find
in this nether world?
The mystery of being a grebe?
Sustenance?
Maybe they are the same.

He reappears somewhere else,
disturbing the lake for only a moment.

This is life, this is truth
for the one who is awake.

cartesian non-sense

"I think
therefore I am,"
said Descartes.
The twit!

What about
non-human "ams"
who can't articulate
their isness?

Are *they* **not**?

lament

I awake and reach
for a book at my side,
lose myself in poetry,
awash in Mary Oliver's
reflections on our wildly natural world.

She and I are a vanishing species.
The eyes of the world are riveted,
trained upon the shopping mall
and all its treasures, on the rigid
geometry of city, on the shallowness
that passes for
life as we dwindle in front of
flickering screens of several kinds
and negate, ignore, despoil what is
truly alive, what breathes us!

> Who shall read the heron's lines?
> Who shall direct the owl's flight?
> Who shall film the rain's downpour
> or record the small snow's drift?

We bear the script
in our hands, the story
in our bodies, but we
are a species gone
astray. We've washed up
on an iron shore with
no place left to go.

new lease

The earth *will*
restore herself
after we leave off
ravaging her and
vanish, leaving only
God's dream of us
with God.

She will return
and like a mother
offer herself yet again
to life, to a species
still unknown but one
that will cling more closely
and hold more dearly
her inimitable gifts.

ii. “what are you doing here, elijah?”

first

Before manifestation

silence brooded,
pervasive throughout
the dark hollow of space
ripe with infinite
possibility

then without warning
for the very first time
the curtain was rent
sending fiery flame
abroad
and God came forth
from all eternity.

day

When the many-layered darknesses of night
peel back,
shapes emerge
inchoate, unclear.

Slowly, steadfastly
a tree takes form,
a mountain range appears.

Colors come to birth with time
beginning dully,
increasingly intense.
The lake's water pearls silvery
beneath a puff of cloud.

This is the gift
of God's First Day when
God's heart turned over with delight
in the fine fire of creation.

and god said

And God said, "Let humankind arise from the earth, with eyes to see to the very depth of things, and ears tuned to the song I place within you, the music all creation sings. And so, with eyes that truly see and ears that truly hear, you will love and honor, protect and guard, nurture and cultivate life and beauty wherever you find it: in those of my creatures that make their home in the deep waters; in those that ply the currents of the air on the strength of their wings alone; in the little ones whose tunnels disappear beneath your feet, and in the beasts whose very size and wildness frighten you.

All those who dwell on earth shall acknowledge in each other and taste within themselves the preciousness of life, with the invitation TO BE: to be both lover and beloved, as am I. For I AM WHO I AM. That is my name. And my name is your name. I share it with you."

Genesis 1:26-31

i wonder if

I wonder if
gurus and guides
have it wrong.
Breath is not
a vehicle to
get from here to there.
Breath is It
and always Is,
always creating
the cosmos in
the eternal *now*.
We breathe a while
but Breath goes on
and on
and
. . .

welcome

Overtaken by I AM
I am stopped
encountered
awakened

Overshadowed by I AM
I am questioning
fearful
going deeper

Overcome by I AM
I am all come apart
open, exposed
breathless yet breathing

I AM
like a pent-up stream
overtakes
overshadows
overcomes
comes over

comes upon
comes in
IS HERE.

work

The calm, serene
and beautiful
are spiritual goals
to be acquired.

We accept them
without question,
berate ourselves
whenever we fail.

But could it be
that sparks and fire
of friction and struggle
are holy work?

Within the cauldron
of God's fierce labor
serene and searing
might come together.
They might just be
the same hot breath
of the creative Sacred.

spiritual direction moment

When angular limbs
        fall into place
and twisted features
        start to unfold
his gaze softens
        eyes darken
her face blurs
        suffused with tenderness
(at last, tenderness for self,
        for one's own experience.)

Then I catch my breath
        as the Spirit whispers, "Now...
now is the time...."
        I hold myself in readiness
for the birth about to take place.
        Lovingly, carefully, together we
move to create safe passage
        for the beautiful child.

Welcome, dear one. Welcome.

outside/inside

I wait.
I watch.
I listen.
Meanwhile,
like a voyeur
my focus is
on other people's experience.
Like an eavesdropper,
I listen at the door
of other people's lives.
Will it rub off on me,
their encounter with the Holy?
Am I living vicariously,
hoping to recapture moments when
(how crazy!)
I thought You were mine?

Beloved,
your heart moves
within my heart,
so conformed to its rhythm and pulse
that there is no difference.
You await me at each outbreath,
rush in with every mouthful of air.
How could I ever doubt You
when I meet You over and over again
as my body settles into
and assumes the shape
of prayer.

the sower
a different parable

Each day I go out to sow
casting bits of me onto the ground:
ground that is rich and dark and receptive,
earth that is cracked and dry,
mud that sucks at me like quicksand,
dunes that slither away like serpents,
sculpting themselves into different forms,
even their location shifting with the wind.

Each day I gather what remains
like manna
and in the hollowed, hallowed spaces of Spirit,
put myself together again.
Careful fingers find the pattern
though wind and weather
do their work so well, at times
it's hard to recognize the parts.

No matter.
Each day *I am*
and I become a new configuration,
sower and sown, sinking more deeply
into the earth prepared by the Sacred.

a spiritual direction story

spiritual direction

I see you through the lattice-work
  of your laced fingers, wet with grief:
the weeping, wounded being
  who trusts me with her raw
and jagged edges, and I wonder,

who appointed me
to be in this place with you?

Who made me the treasurer of your tears,
  the bursar of baleful glances?
Who invited me to gaze upon
  this queue of monuments, moments of despair?
Who asked me into your Holy of Holies
  where you lie prostrate before God?

I hug the shadows
  in deference and in awe.
Then I recall the person
  who asked his friends to be with him
as he cried to God in a garden.

I know who calls, who appoints,
who shares the suffering,
who bathes the wounds and honors the pain.
He is here with us.

treasure in the field

If you have a face
I cannot see it
but sometimes catch an echo of faint laughter
and upon reflection realize
I came in just as you were leaving,
felt the wind of your clothing flying
out behind you as you passed.

I go to see what you have left me.
What is the gift this time?
Before me lies
a raw and clumsy patch of ground
suffused in shadows,
quite unknown.

My taste for you intensifies.
Rolling up my sleeves I set to work,
looking for the clues you love to drop.
In the life you place before me
dark earth starts to pulsate
shadows emit sparks.
What seemed clumsy radiates
a mesmerizing charm.
Joy bubbles up through the cracks
as we uncover the treasure
and once again
I fall in love
with you
Creator
of this enchanted universe.

a spiritual direction story

guru

As for me
I will take
the Great Blue Heron
for my teacher.

He is a model
of devotion,
solemn, silent,
singularly focused.
Modestly blending
with rocky shoreline,
he stands tall and still,
humbly permitting
the breeze's teasing
of his fringed tonsure
and his tasseled bib.

Every moment
the Great Blue blesses
everything that is:
water and fishes,
seabirds and sky.

Is there a wiser
spiritual guide?

gifts

The gift of clouds
is mist and rain.

The gift of mist and rain
is limited vision.

The gift of limits
is the ability to focus
on the near
and the now.

The gift of focus
is the gift of being,
of presence,
of self.

The gift of being
is realized divinity.

voices

I sit at the very edge of the lake
bone weary after an arduous hike.
The grebes are snoozing, heads tucked in
after elaborate, lengthy preening.
I close my eyes, receive on my face
the warmly westering sun.
Behind closed lids there is an orange glow
and a silver shimmer of water.

Hear the many voices of my prayer:
the musical clucking of water
over stone, onto sand.
Wind that comes up,
rising slowly, rolling through the tops of trees.
The deep hoarse call of the raven
in its flight across the valley.
The guttural croak of a dry tree
that leans against more limber ones,
creaking and whimpering
in a light breeze.

These are the voices of my prayer.
These are the voices of my God.

tree pose

Sometimes
when I stand in tree pose
the universe converges
upon a single point.
The mirror casts back my reflection
but I see nothing at all,
aware only of the molten flow
that holds me there,
that whirls up my spine
like a dervish dance.

When the trembling starts inside
I wonder whether *this* time
my finite body hosting
this universal outpouring
of energy will hold,
or will it snap, shattering
into a million pieces?

Perhaps that's how Elijah
complete with chariot and horses
disappeared in a moment of time,
atoms scattered throughout the cosmos,
no longer able to contain
the Breath that breathed him into being,
consumed by the Passion that is God.

the tree pose is a yoga pose

breath (1)

When breath finds me home
body and spirit connect
the Divine and Creation merge.

When attention marries breath
awareness drops down
silently observing depth of space.
An inner journey unfolds.
The body speaks in subtle detail.
Ribs separate as lungs fill
and roll together e-a-s-e-fully
when I exhale.
Muscles grow and gather.
Breath, the staff of life,
stands me up in my center.
It evokes intelligence from every cell.
I feel my blood in arms and fingers
inside my legs and in my foot soles,
sensations intimate and yet mysterious
and at the same time completely real.

Breath facilitates fit.
Bones come together as in Ezekiel's dance,
strong, aligned, and stable.

Breath finds the rhythm of the universe.
When it expands at the top and
pools at the base,
I join the movement of the stars
and I am not out of step.

oblation

Heat beats
on my head
creates fear

Flames eat forests
fiery inferno
Rumors of Armageddon
cloud my brain
race through
my dreams

Life is furnace
burning off
the non-essential
leaving what
is dear to God:
naked breath
stripped spirit
ours to offer
ours to give

i am

I am
made of the stuff of stars
with a core of molten fire,
energy ever pressing out
contained by bone,
soft tissue, silent rivers,
a fine cover of skin.

Dropping into that hot interior
with awareness, pure and pointed,
I touch upon the risk of explosion,
great streams of lava,
fragments spattering far and wide
over the darkened universe.

When I traverse
that searing inferno,
emerging on the other side,
the world is perfectly transparent
and I know who
I am.

not a word

Speak me no pious nonsense
when the bush bursts into flame,
thunderclouds pile on Mt. Horeb,
Jesus twists in agony
upon the upraised beam.

Speak not at all
when fire threatens
to singe my hair,
a deluge crashes
around my shoulders,
when Jesus screams
inside of me.

You do not know,
cannot imagine,
beauty that wounds,
passion that burns,
terror, when faced with
the fierce love of a just God
who cannot reject
a murderous people.

godbearer

"Hail, oh favored one…"

Is this what it means to be so favored?
    I cannot see my feet for my swollen belly.
    My effortless walk has become a waddle.
    My breasts drip without warning.
    At last when I have grown accustomed
    to sharing my body with somebody else,
    birth tears me asunder.

Once deserted.

I am no longer one, but two.
I nurture, cultivate, provide,
and lose my heart to you,
only to watch you grow away,
    far-away look in your glance,
    unfathomable depth in your silence.
Into the desert you disappear.
Now God must be your mother.

Twice deserted.

Later, when I come to find you
you are nurturer and provider
to a host of others, courting danger and disaster
till at last they capture you.

Thrice deserted
at your dying, you are wrenched away

from me once more.
Am I to be comforted then
with a resurrected Lord…,
my son?

Is this what it means to be so favored?

Luke 1:28 & 30

cana wine

He was dancing with the bride
    when he became aware of her,
unobtrusive at his side.
    They have no more wine, she said.

And the dance came to a halt
    as he looked into her face,
saw her eyes speak worlds of love,
    cosmic beckoning in the deep space
of Creation.

Filigrees of fear, of wonder,
    plucked like fingers at his heart.
Lady, (and it sounded like
    he was addressing royalty),
it is not my time.

His gaze remaining locked with hers,
    he saw within the wet depth
of her woman's tears, himself:
    upwelling, surging, and emerging
in a second birth.

Is it? was his whisper
    and it hung between them, quivering.
Then he caught her, strong embrace,
    and turned to seek his Father's face
before opening the door
    to the beginning of his life,

the outpouring of himself
    in this, the first of many signs.

Cana wine.

John 2

i will not worship you

I will not worship you.
I will not look at you,
your eyes cast heavenward
in mute acceptance
of an untimely end,
hanging, limbs akimbo,
in your agony of plaster,
marble, wood and glass
while faithful pilgrims
prostrate themselves in
endless procession through the ages,
knees grinding into the ground.

  Was this your intention?
  Was this your desire?

I will not worship you
but as your follower and friend,
will lead you through the temples,
ask you, well-worn whip in hand,
to rid us of the idols
and the images, all that obscures
the Holy One whose nearness you proclaimed.

What if
  before beginnings
    God only desires that
      we "come and see,"
        spend seventh-day, sabbath time together,
          to behold and marvel that Creation
            is very, very good?

What if
before beginnings
God's only desire
is not to be worshipped
but to be loved?

holy

I AM in the burning bush
Named at last, you, I
You, Yahweh, I, I am, I AM

I hear your voice and,
shoes in hand,
eyes on holy ground
I dare not look up.
It is too bright
to see.

Sent I am.
I AM sends
me.
Sends me to deliver
into freedom.
Named and sent
I am. I AM

The burning bush,
now a smoking cross,
I hear your voice and,
shoes in hand, eyes on holy ground,
I cannot look up.
It is too dark
to see
on the cross

I AM

Named

Sent **Given**

Delivered

into

Freedom

Exodus 3

here to stay

A splash of sunlight
  plays upon the feet of Jesus
    on the cross in the chapel.

How often have I sat here
  in front of your enigmatic figure,
    my mind alternately seething,
      or empty of all things,
        apparently lifeless?

But it's always the same with you,
  isn't it? You're never going to climb down and
    treat me like one of those lambs that got lost,
      carry me on your shoulders or
        cradle me in your arms,
          place your hands upon my head,
            or call me "woman," let alone "daughter."

If you think you can discourage me
  with your static expression
    and your dead silence,
      with your protruding bones
        or your grotesque dance upon that splintered wood,
Forget about it.

I'm going to sit here
till hell freezes over
or the flames learn a different trade.

daffodils

On Friday
my lover brought
an indifferent bunch
of bowed green stalks,
each stalk ending in
a thin brown hood
holding the flower captive.

I had little faith
that they would open,
so disconsolate did they look.

I kept vigil
all that Friday
but saw little change.

The unfolding began reluctantly
in stillness, without fanfare.
Not till Easter did daffodils burst
into the fullness of trumpet song
accompanied by scent so sweet
it might have lured Jesus from his tomb,
held him back from his ascension,
to bury his face once more in
a wealth of ochre blooms,
bouquet of earth's abundance.

choose life

What happens when the invitation
to celebration becomes an act
of alienation?

What happens
when words turn to straw on my tongue
and stick in my throat
and my voice chokes
on the dust of long-dead hymns;
when my heart withers
from lack of nourishment
and my body, distorted
with the effort to conform,
cries out, "No more!
This is not my experience.
This is not my reality."

What is happening?

I am garbed in hypocrisy
and falseness is my daily bread.

The road to authenticity is a lonely one.
Or so I thought.
When feet find themselves upon it,
however falteringly,
and eyes begin to focus
in the unfamiliar light
I see ahead a ragtag band
of others: street people,

women,
lost ones,
run-aways.
Walking congenially among them,
an arm around one, laughter shared with another,
is the One who sees through labels,
changes words, sings a song to
the tune of his own reality,
welcoming folks back to theirs.

He waits for me.

litany

Men in skirts.

Enabling women
        polishing brass
        for men in skirts
                        and burned at the stake

        laundering linen
        for men in skirts
                        and burned at the stake

        baking bread
        for men in skirts
                        and burned at the stake

Good for ordering
the household of God
                        good for the stake

Forever locked
out of circles of sanctity.
Only men in skirts
can mediate God
and women are good
                        for burning,

for the burning
under men's skirts
                        for burning at the stake.

Some things are only good
for burning.

Maybe the church
is one of them.

journey
(in the way of Ignatius)

We watch them till they are mere specks
on a wide and vacant desert:
woman huddled in her shawl
jouncing on the donkey's back,
man beside her, walking tall,
into Egypt.

I say to you, let us go too.
Let us start upon this journey
into unknown lands and future
where we have no friends, no home,
no kin waiting, no work to perform.

At our feet I see two backpacks,
royal blue, festooned with straps
of leather and with shiny buckles.
Bulging with their contents,
they are equal size and weight,
heavy with the same provisions.

As I hand one on to you
and I look into your eyes
I know you pack no miracles.
I can expect no angel bands
or acts of God along the way:
just all things needed for the voyage
and your priceless company

until we reach that other country,
an extraordinary banquet,
that long promised feast.

Matthew 2:13 &14

Ignatian prayer: St. Ignatius of Loyola left us a prayer practice which involves the use of one's imagination with scripture passages.

what magdalene heard

"Let go,
do not cling
to me, I am on
my way, already
I am no longer whom
you know and soon I
shall be scattered to
the wind,
to *Ruah.*
You will find me
everywhere
throughout the cosmos,
sifted like manna
upon the earth,
food for all.
I will return
to you,
look for me,
I am yours
in your breath
till your last breath when
you will dance with me
throughout the cosmos,
sifted like manna
upon the earth,
food for all."

John 20

the labyrinth

It's a disaster from the start.
I'm forced to turn left
when I prefer right
and worm-like, sinuous
paths painted green
on crude canvas flooring
trap me, squeeze me, full as I am
of words meant only for God.

Short, tortured trails,
breath-stopping switchbacks
become a ribbon, wondrously long
flowing deeply into the room,
a place transformed
where sunlight spills
through a garden-gazing window.

Walking back is easy, light.
I scarcely touch the floor.
I dance, I skip, I float upon
a sea of grace, of gratitude.
On this tide I'm swept outside
where Nature paints the labyrinth.

people who sit

I was looking for people
  who sit
so I went to sit with the Buddhists.
I was told to bow
when I crossed the room
to the images of the elders.

I was looking for people
  who sit
so I went to sit with the Quakers.
I was cushioned in silence
when someone spoke—
of books and films and shopping malls.

I was looking for people
  who sit
so I went to my room
and closed the door,
sat down on my prayer stool
and there they were:
the people who sit
all over the world.

beloved

Beloved
You who dwell
at the heart of Creation,
come
and make yourself known to us.

Give us this day
life in its fullness.
Forgive us when we
deny it in others
as we forgive those
who take it from us.
Keep us from hopelessness
and despair and deliver us
into freedom.

For you are life
and breath, body
and being in
every moment's
eternity.
Amen.

sitting

In the dark
of this overcast morning
rain dribbling down my window
like a constant refrain
I sit on my prayer bench
knees nailed to the floor
and behind closed lids
see a series of images
hundreds of me's
sitting on benches
always the same
forever and ever.

I consent to this ageless sitting
this timeless time
in which I am always sitting
sit eternally
committed to
the Eternal One.

contemplation

My eyes work overtime
straining to penetrate and grasp
    somehow
the Other.
I want the inner,
the invisible,
the profundity of depth and center.

When eyes let go their greedy desire
and effort falls away at last,
the sacred core of things reveals itself.
The Holy does not hold back
but welcomes me, enveloping me like breath,
like mist, and I am changed.
Like knows like in space without limits,
in form without boundaries.
Nothing separates You and me.

take my heart

Take my heart, Beloved.
Take it now.
Pluck it out of its cage
and take it to Yourself,
or I will stand here
forever
come wind, rain, snow,
with Tekarra veiled,
Cavell disappeared,
a storm coming down the valley.
The circumstances are a matter of indifference to me.
Take my yearning heart
Beloved.
Take it now.
I offer it.
It is yours.

Mt. Tekarra and Mt. Edith Cavell
are peaks in Jasper National Park

a poet's prayer

I went to pray
but did not pray,
read poetry instead;
my body soft,
my breath expansive,
landing deep
within the space
where thought has yet to form.

Like dew, like light,
like spidery web,
the Holy covers me.

I shudder with
its intimacy.
I tremble at
its vastness.

I went to pray
and did not pray.

Poetry prayed me.

prayer at providence

In my moth-mind,
moth-wings flicker
scattering moth dust.
Furry bodies
thrash and flail.
Thoughts, though many,
do not hold me.
Underneath
I hear the radiant
quiet of a temple
now at rest.

Providence Retreat Center

breath (2)

My breath is
a stairway to the stars.
Suspended from heaven,
unfurling slowly,
it is like heavy drapery,
fold by fold dropping down,
dropping down
endlessly.

Then,
(oh magic moment)
breath becomes still.
I am surrendered to the silence.
When breath quiets
I touch apparent nothingness,
eternity opens up within.

Desire to remain, to dwell, is interrupted
by the soft spontaneous rising of the breath
as if from nowhere
unbidden, unwilled, but ever so.
It climbs up repeatedly
and inevitably descends again.

Perhaps they are the same,
the up and down, the height and depth.
When at last my breath shall cease
all will be revealed.
Eternity will receive me,
and I will not be back.

unconsoled

Breathing into
the raw wound of
the unconsoled, its
ragged edges waving
like wind-blown petals,

each small breath
scalding the naked,
pulsing, yearning
heart   broken
open and weeping
for the Beloved...

how
is one to endure it?

Inspired by James Finley's book, *Christian Meditation*

all

This is all there is…
the breath
and the un-breath

organic breath

With your breath, Beloved,
grow me
strong and true
not a light whiff
that evaporates
but organic breath
incarnate,
rising deep
within my center
rooted, sturdy
like a tree
yearning upwards
bursting into
a banquet of leaves
spreading thick and wide.

With your breath
standing me up
I can be in the world
awake and aware
gifted and giving
in face of so much
bleakness.

spirit

Being born again
a free fall
a tall tumbling
held only by the wind
that blows wherever it pleases

Born of the wind,
born of the breath,
borne by breath,
breathed by wind,
knowing nothing
but wind, but breath
coming
going
gone

So it is with those born of the Spirit

John 3

day after day

Day after day
I tend the absence of God.
Perched precariously on the edge
leaning now into the great nothing
and then again pulling back,
I grow accustomed to dis-ease,
accept the unsettled nature of this grace.
The struggle, however, to maintain at least
a likeness of balance has left me with
a raw disposition and brittle bones.
My spirit knows little rest,
my tears have no weight,
leaving scarcely a trail
on my heart's dry ground.

I will not desert you
O Spacious One,
though within me the lack
of your presence resounds.
Expand and stretch me
until one day I might
find comfort in
your limitlessness.

spaciousness

spaciousness
graciousness of space
clarity of perspective
economy of lines
un-clutter
Silent surfaces
open
free
Inviting, hospitable:
celebrating possibility
of presence,
of listening
to the inscape,
the unfolding into
the expanse of
ah!
divinity
duskly dancing,
brightly pearling
centered and pouring
through

"vast emptiness, nothing holy"

When questions cease to
plague me
and answers matter
even less
I don't know who I am
I don't know who God is
and I am not
lost.

Title is from a koan, as quoted by John Tarrant
in *Bring Me the Rhinoceros*

"what are you doing here, elijah?"

Horeb was a long way off,
the wilderness entangled me.
I thought I was equipped to meet
the demons but the conflict
left me weak.

I dropped my tools
(what use were they?)
to climb the mountain,
hoping for a blessing,
presence, maybe a tablet
or two or three…

Pummeled instead by heavy winds,
by hail, by lightning, I lost my ground.
Face down in the dust
I caught the sound
"of sheer silence."

I wrapped it around me
like a cloak. I wore it
on the descent.
The gift of it still
astonishes me but
slowly now and carefully
I make a home for Silence.

1 Kings 19:12

nameless

I will not use your name again.
The Hebrews had it right.
I'll tend the silence. If I speak,
it will be vastness, no-thingness,
        incomprehensibility.
My childish rantings will recede
and echo faintly in the void.
Only Mystery can name mystery.
All I can do is remove my shoes.

promise

You shall live
in the Great Silence
between the Unknown
and the known.

In this contradictory balance
you shall find my Peace.

iii. to write or not to write

gift for a writer

Grace consists of a window seat,
spring's mellow sun upon my neck,
a view over trees heavy with blooms
and water, changing ever with
each shift of wind and variation
of light, my belly filled
with depth of silence
open to the mystery,
mystery that comes to me
on softly-padded, slippered feet
most surely when I wait.

plath and sexton

Neither heaven nor hell
is my habitat.
How then can I
be a poet?

Suicide is not something I contemplate,
it is not on my schedule
nor in my repertoire.
It does not call me from afar.
How then can I be a poet?

I am not prone to mental illness,
nervous breakdowns are alien to me.
My life is not lived
on the razor's edge.
How then can I be a poet?

But wait.
Perhaps it is the poet in me
who rebels, who flails
at deadly traditions,
rigid institutions,
passive negativity.
And because I walk the periphery,
with one foot in, the other out,
woman on the margins,
I am a poet.

Sylvia Plath and Anne Sexton are both poets who committed suicide.

other voices

They troop in
soon as I dare
to raise my voice,
speak less-than-nice
words, or images that
flare into flame.

> "You can't say that.
> What will they think?
> There goes your reputation!"

Ancient voices
from sites long buried;
strong and active
nevertheless
and chanting like
a backstage chorus.

> Compassionate, gentle, and serene:
> so I am perceived.
> Not angry, loud, sarcastic, bitter.
> Yet these are voices that want out!

What a risk
to let them speak.

What risk
to keep them captive.

protesting poet

Every poet who is a poet
has written protest poems.

Every poet who protests
is mothered by
the quest for truth
and for a world
that's just.

Am I called
to join their ranks,
utter views that contradict,
speaking for the silent hordes
or for the least lost tribe,
for *me*?

I am poet.

Every poet who is a poet
has to write protest poems.

for denise levertov

You are a beacon
or more likely
you are Eve
extending the
forbidden apple
to my uncertain hands.
Shall I bite it,
taste its sweetness,
let its juice run
down my fingers,
shall I accept its omen?

"Speak, woman!
Speak *woman!*
Don't deny
a cell, a single fiber.
Raise your voice,
though cracked with age,
raw from neglect
yet one with women
who had their voices
torn, unraveled,
prematurely hushed.
Or found them
whole and generative,
in their wisdom years."

Take my sticky, fruit-full hand
Denise,
I want you
by my side.

summer eucharist

Toe to toe
in a tiny garden
we sat among asters
and fading daisies
with an old grey cat
weaving mutely through
our casually planted legs.

Shadows lengthened.
The sun trailed westward.
We stepped inside
and went on talking,
musing quietly,
at times uncovering
unplumbed passions,
greater depth.

Nibbling on berries
and birthday cake
we read poetry,
spoke theology,
slipping easily into silence,
blessed by one another's presence.

Five friends gathered,
holy, and holding
sacred space
for body and soul.

poetry time

Waking on a Sunday morning
hanging on to half a dream
 I know this will be
 poetry time.

Rising to the top of slumber
various times throughout the night
to the sound of rain swizzling
down the drainpipe I
knew this would be
 poetry time.

Day breaks virginal before me
not a scratch or murmur on it,
nothing to attract or distract
just the visceral pull inside
 to sit beside the inner well
 awaiting the inevitable stir,
 bubbles rising to the surface,
 popping open, blossoming.

night rain

Burrowed deep in my bed
I hear the rain fall
weightily in the garden,
sweep the roof with galloping gusts,
indifferent to my plight.

I fall asleep with poems
dropping from the sky,
caught beyond my eyelids
by nocturnal leafy arms.

All night long they murmur.
In the morning I awake
with poetry on my lips.

to write or not to write

It's all right
not to write.

Being present
to sun-warmed earth,
to towering clouds,
to sea-salt air,
to the gull's lament
is more than enough.

No need to write
at all.

poems

Each time a poem presents itself,
comes shuttling shyly from the shadows,
it carries within it endless gifts,
a chest overflowing with treasure.
Before it appears to be truly complete
it will have tried on many costumes,
gone through various metamorphoses
before it finds its home.

The process is play,
delight the poet's work,
as she tastes words and phrases,
sifts through images,
dances with placement,
toys with commas
and in the final winnowing,
discards everything extra.

In the end
the poem knows
exactly what it means to be.
As phrases meet and images blossom
the poem takes root
and the poet knows
she has been the usher
of a fragment of eternity.

natalie

She's unfocused
and distracted,
her eye caught
by any movement;
constantly derailed
by a mercurial mind
that runs with every thought and image,
barely landing, scarcely taking
an unencumbered breath.

It's easy for me to criticize.
I write at whim. She labors
and has, over her craft,
long years, many hours.

When I shake myself
out of her book
I drop into the web,
that universal conflagration
of intersecting points,
that unalterable connectedness
which she, good student of Zen,
sees, feels, tries to describe.

Lodged still deeper
than the author's art
is the timeless sitting of zazen
where even the cosmic web dissolves.
Connections melt, are gathered up

in the vastness of
the One.

She knows.

For Natalie Goldberg, author

zazen: a meditation practice

poem

Every poem is many poems
has lived multiple lives
known myriad forms.

Who decides its final version
and who's to say that others,
now discarded,
did not also wish to be?

In a universe in which nothing is lost
discarded poems throng the air,
penetrate leaves and petals,
skin and hair,
join with poems never written,
never thought, but lived.
So the cosmos regenerates,
a poem without bounds.

attendance

In the glow cast by her poem
I hold very, very still.
Awe and wonder, stinging tears
visit me like welcome friends.

Silence grows up from my foot soles,
rises in my legs to settle
deep within my inner self.
From the womb my breath receives it,
welcomes it and carries it
like a cloud throughout my heart
quietly, my spirit waiting,
listening with a delicate ear.

Behold the blessing of attending.
This is when the world discloses
all its secrets (are they secrets?),
is created in an instant,
in a pulse of timelessness.
Now, now, forever, *now*.

inner poet

When the inner poet speaks
she comes from long ago:
from the fecund silence of the world's womb,
from the profundity of eons spent
nurturing and brooding
over the merest speck, the slightest trace.

The passage from silence to speech
can be perilous, fraught with danger.
The treasure she labors over
is so easily lost, so quickly broken.
The path is tangled and obscure
or suddenly comes to an end.
Then she must find another way.

In the fullness of her creative powers
she forges and carves and shapes
like the forces that kneaded the earth.
Lifting and surging and sure
she secures the world for God.

the power of poetry

Oh, it's raining, snowing, I don't know which
as I bite off a piece of poetry
and let it roll around inside me where
it blends with darkness, softness,
edginess and, ahhh, drops,
drops so deep it's like a free-fall
and it gently, oh so gently, opens something
like a wound ....

I try but cannot stay
with that huge openness for long.
I have to put the book aside
sit very still with the
great rush of the cosmos
that has just passed through.

poet laureate

The Poet Laureate's term is up.
Who will take his place?
I nominate
the Great Blue Heron
whose poetic scrawls
are written in sky,
huge oblong wings
sketched on ocean air,
whose statuesque stance
at water's edge
evokes deep pools
of stillness.

I nominate the Great Blue Heron,
the nation's Premier Poet.

poetry and poets

Early in the morning
left alone in our snug home
I seek my bed, still warm,
still bearing my impression
and I wander through a book
of poems, wondering how
simple words in certain order
strip me, lay my innards bare.

A landscape lies within me
where the heart weaves mystery
and luminous ribs appear like
coral beneath a shallow sea and
deeper yet the womb brings forth
dark herbs and spices by the searching
light of words.

Poets listen, live between
the inner and the outer world,
search the thread that knits them close,
spin it into something new.

a reading

Gathered in a cozy home
on an early summer eve
we sip green tea in large glass cups
exploring easy conversation.

I am first to read,
a quartet whose instruments sing
the birthing of poem and poet.
The coda is unmeasured silence,
not uncomfortable
but quite impossible to track.

Not until the next day
do I feel the alien again,
a stranger in a foreign land.
What had I been looking for,
what did I want to hear?
A deep sigh, perhaps a heartfelt
"Yes, that's how it is."
Not this unwelcome loneliness.

As I brood over my emptiness,
lightly rocking, cradling myself,
a small grace sails slowly by.
It wants my attention, it almost waves!
I see, I note, I let it land. And this is it:
    Poetry is *my* gift of tongues,
    love language meant for God alone.

food

Sitting in
a sunshine window,
skin singing with warmth
I am infinitely content,
and deeply grateful
for a crusty slab,
thickly buttered,
of sourdough bread
from a sturdy round loaf,
a mug of tea,
hot and strong,
and for Mary Oliver's
"Goldenrod," read
in one ecstatic breath
lest it slip through my soul
without burning me.
The bread, the butter, the
"rumpy bunches, saffron
and orange and pale gold"
feed me equally well.
Lit by sky and sea
and briefly shadowed by
a gull in flight, they have the
very same flavor.

too many ghosts

Ghosts.
They waltz, they tango
out of the shadows
when she says,
"Write! From
the beginning.
Where does your story
start?"

In the beginning
was the dance.
Who gave it
to the ghosts?

What a motley crew—
the thin, the crippled,
the bent over,
the one whose neck
is stuck in a noose;
then there is
the transparent one
who would have me believe
I do not exist.

I'm going back to the beginning.
I'm learning how to dance
and like a dervish I'll dance my ghosts
into such a state of bliss that

drunk on God they will lie at my feet,
totally transformed.

After meeting with the Writer-in-Residence
at the University of Alberta.

iv. the seasons of my life

spring geese

I awoke this morning
to a pale March sky
and a wind just waiting
to boil and bluster when

two great shadows
passed overhead
and skidded onto
the lake's thin ice
and stood there
not a foot apart,
honking randomly.

Overjoyed at their coming
I paused to watch.
Had they expected
the soft splash of water
or the wild welcome
of their friends?

Not long after, they were gone
as if it had all been a dream.
The lake stood mute.
I felt bereft.
We both missed the sound
of their lively presence
and had to bow to
winter once more.

april

Buds are eager
  they push to unfold
but snow and cold
  stifle their enthusiasm.
Not yet. Be patient.
  Exercise a little caution,
is the message of the wind
  worrying the stiff, unsupple branches.

"A word to the wise is sufficient,"
  but spring does not heed.
Life wants out, must manifest,
  and so morning comes
and the spindly clematis
  stands shivering in a bank of new snow.
The tulips, in clumps, defy the weather.
  They have each other
for company.
  The buds on the apple trees
keep their own counsel.
  They don't like to hear,
"I told you so."

Life wants out, *will* out,
  when time and the elements are ripe.
For now it is good
  to contain the inner
a little longer in
  what remains of winter's shelter.
Time enough
  for the siren song of spring.

siberian spring

They say this spring
is Siberia's gift.
Well into May
gales buffet our bodies
and heavy-browed skies
spill rain, spit snow.

A stoic hyacinth
stands by the door
as if made of stone,
its growth arrested,
its raw pink petals,
like knuckles, clenched.

Day after day
we tighten ourselves
against the relentlessness
of Nature, she who has formed
a grim alliance
with a season that will not budge.

Our resolve wears thin,
our hearts shrivel
for want of softness,
for tender touch.

Come, come swiftly, spring, come
now, and bring us back to life.

tulips

Tulips
the size of teacups
make me smile all over.
Standing tall
in a crystal vase,
a wide open flower
coaxes me in
to its deep pink interior
at whose base blazes
a black velvet star
radiating an aureole
of bright ochre.
A bead of nectar nestles upon
its night-shade depths.
Near it a waxy stud
resembles an aberrant form
of coral, studded with
spade-tipped threads
  that shudder
beneath my breath.

Were it just a little larger
I would risk bending back
its petals to dip my face
in the bloom's smooth bowl.

Baptism by immersion.

Palm Sunday

berries

Strawberries!
Bright, inviting,
we have them for breakfast
one morning in May.

Crisp as apples
no juice to speak of
their only claim
to the fruit they are named for
appears to be their scarlet hue.

I think of an even
earlier morning.
We rose to witness
a mountain dawn.
Our gaze could not hold
so much beauty for long
and dropped to our feet
where just as lovely
  but miniscule,
wild strawberries grew
on the forest floor.
Too few to collect,
I ate every one
and tasted the sunrise
on my tongue.

dawn

Cars line our winding road
like abandoned toys,
insignificant,
awaiting human contact
to animate them
while the eastern sky,
illumined by dawn,
unmasks the street lamps,
still burning, still wedded
to night.

Nothing stirs
as the scarlet glow thickens,
spills over the edge,
coloring distant clouds.

Street lights pale,
snap off almost audibly,
conceding their poverty
as if on command.

Sunlight slips silently
over the world.
Its wondrous work,
daily repeated,
goes largely unnoticed
by a people asleep.

after the flood

They congregate, they huddle,
shiny black mantles catch the sun.
What ominous plans are hatching
among the crows, the magpies,
the scavengers that have descended
in the days after the flood?

They are the masters now
in their funereal garb,
presiders over death
and devastation of backyard
gardens, abandoned furniture,
junked cars. They prance,
they hop, they jubilate
over our misfortune.

One purple clematis
blooms valiantly on
its shredded vine.

A flood rises
behind my eyes…
at last.

July 18, 2004
Edmonton

july oh-four

Last day of July dawns
cloudy and cool.

July cannot end soon
enough, this month
of pelting rain,
vicious thunder, hellish hail,
and flooded homes.

I will not miss your un-
sunny days of
high humidity, your
tortured nights of
lying awake.

Be on your way and let us hope
eleven months stretch long enough
to ease the impact of your wrath.

swimmer

Somewhere
around the 29th lap
I open my eyes
to a different world.

Gone is concern
for the perfect stroke,
for keeping count,
for "Watch out, the edge!"

The spring-green poplars,
aspens and firs
brighten and shimmer
as buoyant water
slips past my sides,
lifts my arms,
supports my legs.

When I stop holding myself apart
and join the flow of the universe
I find I am part of the grand design
at the innermost core of the world.

turning sixty

Turning 60.
End of midlife
when outspread wings
caught sun, held rain,
answered the lure of always more,
more world, more life, more love.

Wings draw close
to a body marked
with days, with time's
mercurial ways.
I step into
the fall of life,
welcome opportunity
to live the spare,
explore the simple,
marry authenticity.

fallow field

A field lies fallow in early autumn,
shorn and deserted
after harvest.
It stretches as far as I can see,
a carpet of prickly stubble
under a pale indifferent sky.
            The big effort
            the final push
            to come to fruition
            to bear abundantly
has given over to simple being.
It's an ordinary field,
      bumpy and rough,
            nothing more.

The longer I wander here
the more familiar it becomes
and intimacy grows, though I denounce
the uneven ground that makes me stumble,
and curse the sharp stray stalks that cut
and though the loneliness makes me cry ... sometimes.

The resting earth lies quietly
with no expectations, no excuses,
only the certainty that nothing ever stays the same.
More and more I entrust myself
to the unending procession of comings and goings.
I am committed to the seasons of my life.

advent

Each star-blistered moment
  ablaze: the burning bush,
a conflagration, the searing,
  soul-searching emergence of
the Other, the wholly New,
  of the awe-full mystery
named Ineffable...

  given in increments
  carefully, slowly,
  or we would never
  survive its coming.

free for christmas

Christmas in
my jeans!
I feel like a child
that has eluded
the censoring glances
and tight-clipped phrases
of tut-tutting elders.

I'm free
of convention,
of expectation,
free to sit in my chair all morning
writing and reading as much as I like;
free to take a vigorous walk,
pale winter sun
dogging my heels.
I'm cooking for two,
not the usual horde,
and I'll not be persuaded
to change for dinner.

It's Christmas and
I'm wearing my jeans
from morning till night.
At fifty-seven I'm free to choose
how I'll spend this precious day.
I don't want to read
the Christmas story,
I don't want to hear
"Messiah" once more.

I'll speak to our children
on the phone
and hope that the flicker
returns to our yard.

Tomorrow I'll wake,
stretch, and savor
the gift of freedom
that Christmas is
every day of the year.

new mexico

Driving in winter through high desert country
the land everywhere rolls away,
away to an endless horizon.
So stripped, so sere, so full of memories,
it rends my heart and bares my soul.

Once upon a time I lived here.
Then, on the eve of holidays
I'd step onto that worthy beast
known affectionately as the "A T S F"
and travel through fast-gathering dusk
from university, home.

Mauve and purple, peach and sand,
the mountains kept up with the train
till they at last fell back upon
the inky black of night.

The rumbling, rocking car slipped
into silence, drowsy passengers nodding off.
My reading light, a startling cone,
sliced the dark as I settled down,
digging deep into well-worn seat,
sinking into my book.

Now, big old cottonwoods
whose twigs and branches are still dressed
in fall's dry leaves resemble an old
curandera, wrinkled and lined,
feet shuffling to music only she hears,

reaching up her withered arms
as twisted fingers rake the sky.

This land's severe beauty
is plaited with my history.
That story's voice used to ring
in keening wails, a plaintive dirge.
Now its song breaks up on sage
and sand, diffuses over desert vastness,
shimmers in an unblemished sky
and disappears forever.

The *curandera* does her work,
I don't know how or why.
Released from shadows that imprisoned
I ride through this lonely country,
tasting healing in my mouth.

done

I am done
with nostalgia,
clinging vine that it is.

I am done
with sweetness that cloys,
the ecstatic or the tragic
past.

I am done with
wallowing, with blame,
with analyzing yesterdays
to wring out yet another drop
of reason, hope of understanding
people and events long lost
to me and so they *need* to be.

I let them go,
I shall not let
nostalgia resurrect again.

who I am

Who do I say that I am?

I am a woman torn and whole
a woman blessed and blemished
shining, radiant
tarnished, tired.
I am woman.
I am.

Who do You say that I am?

You are woman
heart of my heart
the apple of my eye
the dancer and the dream
I had from the beginning.
With you I build sandcastles
and make mud pies.
With you I chart the heavens
and fling stars into space.
I want to be with you
always.

oyster

I am
an oyster.
Grant me a grain of sand,
cast me a speck of dirt
and I will work it,
weave a web of stuff around it,
create a nest, a home,
a dwelling place for soul.

If nothing is given,
nothing received,
I am lost and set adrift.
Then the labor must begin.
I have to find myself.

The work is dark,
mining in constricted space
and many a tunnel has to be dug
before I see some light.

Trust bypasses the terrible effort.
When I can trust that indeed I am
and am just what God wants me to be
the struggle recedes,
emptiness fills,
loneliness evaporates
while treasure ripens within, flowing forth
to meet a world created in Love.

free

Freedom means
never having to say *I* again,
and in the free fall of *I*-lessness,
flowing into the **I** of God
and recognizing
myself.

Freedom means
never having to *say*
again
and in wordlessness
joining my no-voice
to God's all-speech
and hearing beyond language
the dynamic Word of freedom,
creating form from formlessness,
breathing Being
into the void.

mountain

I would like
to be a pilgrim
ever walking toward
Mt. Kidd, always en route
to its massive shoulders,
its mist-shrouded summit,
its enduring presence.

I would like always
to be so alive, so aware
of the perfect tension
that holds all things
in balance, poised
on the edge of wholeness,
a panorama ever unfolding,
the Holy offered
in sacrament of earth.

mystics

In patient immobility
the mountain waits,
trusting in the growing dawn.
She has watched throughout the night,
never doubting darkness, giving
herself to its abyss-like embrace.
Alone she meets first light.

A small and docile mist
slips easily across the morning water.
The solitary grebe emerges
parting its pliant wings,
creating ever-expanding circles
as he explores, without a sound,
the nether regions of the lake.
He knows what it is
to companion darkness and dawn,
and is as faithful to their difference
as the stalwart steady mountain.

Mountain and mist,
water and grebe:
to be a mystic is not to be
anything other than what one is.

less

I have less and less to say.
Don't want to explain
brevity or justify
silence. Less is steady,
strong and true, reliable
witness to Mystery.

star

A star stands out straight
from my kitchen window.
When I gaze at it long enough
it begins a dithery dance,
bobbing up and down,
side to side
upon the thick night sky.

Or is it actually I
who lose my balance
and end up flying
around the room?

In the darkness
who would ever know,
who will ever tell?
Not I!

daft

This is a promise

I'll grow more daft
wandering
from pillar to post
leaving the bed made
only halfway
in order to write
a poem
leaving the dinner
unattended
as I sink deeper
focusing closely
into a yoga pose
fragmented
because the inner
voice has become
so insistent
I must pay
attention.

Thank goodness I have
Jung in my corner
who claims
the second half of life
involves just that:
the call inside.

So I'll continue
to grow more daft

and do so with
authority!

don't look to me

Don't look to me
for methods or teachings,
for wisdom or illumination.
I have nothing to offer now
but my self receiving my life
and learning how
to be.

what, not why

Why
does not matter
anymore.
Like arrows whizzing
through the air,
it misses the target
more often than not,
leading astray,
obscuring, entangling
the nimble paths
of mind.

Why
is not a useful word.
It never settles down
to *what.*
What is now, is under foot,
within my hand, beneath my breath.
What is embodied, not ethereal,
life in the present,
courageous and real.

convention

The corporate crowd
swarms into the hall
wrapped in a fog
of expensive cologne,
drones in black,
immaculately groomed,
expressionless faces,
youthful and hard.

In the rec room
two suave accountants
invest their break
in a ping pong game.
Quite uncommitted,
her left hand is thrust
into the pocket of black silk trousers
snugly drawn over lithe hips while
her other hand wields the paddle.
He, not a crease in his armor,
not a hair out of place,
lunges after the tiny ball.
A black Gucci briefcase,
simply elegant,
rests in full view
against a post.

Outside stand the silver chariots,
SUV's lined up in a row,
of these young professionals,
so eager to make

their mark, their million,
to make their uniformly monotone selves
meaningful.

death or life?

At sixteen I woke up
to a world in love with death
and set myself against it:
  the blasphemy of the Berlin Wall,
  the Gulag, ABM's.

Half a century later,
a speck in the eye of time,
another wall is raised
this time in the holy land.
The world is still in love with death,
has learned nothing about life's sweetness
from the Vietnam War, Bosnia, Rwanda,
from Agent Orange, PCB's, global warming.

At sixty I still gather steam,
productive anger that informs
my protest and my poetry.
Though nearer to my own demise
I set myself against global death,
  the only way to live.

escape

"L'Escapade."
How aptly named
this exclusive dining room
in a hotel situated
on a mountain top
with a view of God's country.

Dinner, madame, starts with
consommé, sparkling
in a high stemmed glass
planted among thick folds
of a napkin placed
on a heated plate.
A strawberry sorbet
to cleanse the palate
is followed by
potato-artichoke griddle cakes
with portobello mushrooms nestled
among scalloped baby squash, two or three
asparagus spears, a scattering of
roasted red peppers.

I think of war-torn Kosovo;
towns and countryside ripped up,
women raped, children lost,
husbands abducted
or simply murdered.

I live in a time-warp
where people worry

about a second 4-wheel drive,
another Time Share,
a holiday in Cancún or
maybe just Vancouver.

People of Iraq,
beaten down daily
by a cruel embargo,
sicken, starve, and die.

How long will we refuse
to notice, how long will
we cling to this charade
as if to say,
"God desires abundant life
for all, but He really meant
it *just for us.*"

war chant

Men at war
prey upon women

Men at war
women their prey

De-brained, un-souled
their only power
between their legs

"weapons of mass destruction"

Men at war
prey upon women

Not just women
Other men
Children too

All
victims of war and destruction

companion

Sometimes I see
Lady Death
playing
at the corners
of my eyes.

Friendly presence,
she doesn't ask much.
Nevertheless
I stop to ponder
the mystery of being
and not.

I acknowledge her quietly,
consent to her company.
She grows more familiar
with each season.

At the last,
with little fuss,
I hope to follow her
home.

death

Death stalked me yesterday
though heaven knows
I had no hint she was so near.

You were away and I,
when you did not return,
felt Time, my ancient enemy,
sink its claws into my back,
rend the fabric of my calm,
force me to my knees till death
sat full within my throat.
My inner eye saw desolation,
unimaginable grief.

When I heard you on the stairs,
death stepped aside,
for now.

There was another then
who sat across from me
with eyes sunk into face so drawn,
eyes whose darkened density
allowed no light, who spoke
of death as temptress yet
he wanted not to choose her
though his suffering was great.

We had no easy answers,
nothing fell into our hands
but as we sat with death between us

something changed so we could leave her
though we each would have to say
that death, the uninvited stranger
left her calling card that day.

morning and evening poems

When night ends too soon
in the grey wash of dawn
poetry

Kapalabhati
powerful bellows
dark morning dew
falls in silence

Sundown
fire in the west
meets in the east
a flame-filled tree

I was not here
I am here
I will be gone
grace

kapalabhati: powerful, rhythmic breathing associated with yoga and meditation.

tree

Within me grows
a slender tree
whose twigs
reach every part
of me.
It holds me up,
my flesh is draped
on branches
springing from its core.
It breathes me,
blissful breath,
a path of light
and liveliness.

Within me grows
a slender tree
that will in time
become a cross.
No longer strong
with ragged breath
it will give up,
surrender me.

The tree of life,
the tree of death
grow deep within
the heart of me.

exhale

I watch my breath unfurl and like a carpet
just released, roll toward the nether regions
of the room where stands an antique chest of drawers,
polished handles blinking brassy from the darkly
glowing wood. It pours itself into a drawer,
standing open and inviting, snuggling in
as if to take up residence. Not this time.
One day it will roll and roll and pause and stay
and not come back. It will know itself no more.
Not in that form. Not in this place. Not in me.

passion

There are times
unexpected
unlooked for
when the bowl that is me,
bronze and darkly dented,
becomes so brimmed, so pressed, so chafed
with the experience of life
lived fully,
within and without,
at my core and in the cosmos,
that the bottom gives way;
as if the weighty weight
breaks through, wears down
and finds another layer,
a deeper dimension,
still greater capacity.

I am on the way to transparence.
The fullness of love, like a chisel,
creates more space.
This bowl that is me
will be continually carved,
scooped,
worn thin
until its cracked and crazed interior
reveals the fingers of the One who holds it
and I break...
but break into
the hands of God.

the last act

Some day
when the richness of my life
is spent
I will make a final tour,
visit the deep interior
of my incarnate soul,
touching here, resting there,
sipping the few remaining breaths
and then I will let
my breath
go
and
it will be
fine

about the author

ANTOINETTE VOÛTE ROEDER has a Master of Music degree and a certificate from the Pacific Jubilee Program in Spiritual Direction. She is a poet and spiritual director in Edmonton, Alberta, Canada. Antoinette facilitates prayer and meditation and has led retreats and workshops on spirituality and mystics. She has a passion for music, people, and the earth.